The Talk

BY PASTOR RYAN
AND CATHY STORY

WITH CONTRIBUTIONS BY:

PASTOR JAYSON COMBS
PASTOR JOSH COMBS
DR. RANDY T. JOHNSON
PASTOR ROY TOWNSEND

DESIGNED BY: CASEY MAXWELL
FORMATTED BY: SHAWNA JOHNSON

First Edition, February 2023

Published by:
The River Church
8393 E. Holly Rd.
Holly, MI 48442

Scriptures are taken from the Bible,
English Standard Version (ESV)

THE RIVER CHURCH

Printed in the United States of America

CONTENTS

09 LESSON ONE • GOD'S DESIGN IN MARRIAGE

15 Devotion 1: God's Way

17 Devotion 2: Worth the Wait

19 Devotion 3: The Standard of Beauty

21 Devotion 4: The Way They Are

23 Devotion 5: Lost Interest

25 Devotion 6: Just You and Me

29 LESSON TWO • SEX: THE WORD VS. THE WORLD

37 Devotion 1: For Marriage

39 Devotion 2: "And God Saw it was Good"

41 Devotion 3: Let's Talk About it

43 Devotion 4: Interchangeable

45 Devotion 5: Bible Verse for the Bedroom

47 Devotion 6: God's Plan for You

51 LESSON THREE • DANGERS: LITTLE FOXES

59 Devotion 1: Danger of the Grandoise

61 Devotion 2: Danger of Success

63 Devotion 3: Danger of Thoughts

65 Devotion 4: The Beauty of Hardship

67 Devotion 5: Danger of Assuming

69 Devotion 6: Danger of Picking Your Corner

73 LESSON FOUR • DELIGHTS

85 Devotion 1: Remind Them

87 Devotion 2: Who You Are

89 Devotion 3: Delight in Protection

91 Devotion 4: Vertical Delight

93 Devotion 5: Public and Private

95 Devotion 6: Delight

PREFACE

Sex is not a four-lettered word. Although the world and Hollywood have perverted it, sex was designed by God as a gift to be enjoyed within a marriage between a man and a woman. All too often, believers have remained silent concerning the topic of sex in their community, church, and homes. They avoid "the talk."

The topic of sex is so important to God, that there is a whole book of the Bible that discusses the value and importance of it within the beauty of marriage. Preachers have explained the Song of Solomon as a picture of God's love for Israel or as Christ's love for His Bride, the church. Although these are true concepts throughout Scripture, the Song of Solomon is a love story between a man and a woman.

The Talk is divided into four key sections:

- God's Design in Marriage
- Sex: The Word vs. the World
- Dangers: Little Foxes
- Delights

Each section addresses sex openly and respectfully. There are principles discussed that will benefit both the single individual and the married couple.

The Talk consists of four study guides for personal or group discussion and twenty-four devotions for daily instruction. *The Talk* is based on the Song of Solomon. The goal of this book is that we constantly and consistently look to Scripture for guidance in all areas of life including sex.

LESSON ONE

GOD'S DESIGN IN MARRIAGE

PASTOR ROY TOWNSEND

Once I became a homeowner and I had to start doing repairs, it became very clear to me that many of my home's systems were interconnected. There was an overall design. There is a system in place, and often I was hurrying to get a project completed, but then would have to tear out the newly completed work because I forgot to run electricity to that wall, or forgot to run a plumbing lead, or had to wreck something that I had just put in. It became very discouraging because I did not have a good grasp of the overall design and interconnectedness of the systems in the home. I can tell you that it is easier to complete the projects when you understand the overall designs for the project. Well, as we enter the family month with our study of Song of Solomon (Song of Songs), we want to be clear on the designs for marriage within the context of Scripture.

1. Did you ever get into a house project where you did not understand the design or interconnectedness of the project? Please explain what happened.

_____

_____

_____

2. If you were asked what are God's designs or desires for marriage, what would you list?

_____

_____

_____

Daniel Akin writes, "The Song of Songs paints a picture of marital love that reflects the love that instructs us in God's good design and points us to our faithful Shepherd-King, Jesus." So, we can see that the Song of Songs will point us back to Genesis chapters 1-2 to see the original designs, but also project us forward to the marriage relationship depicted in the New Testament. Many of us know that marriage is a gift and a mystery that has a design.

Genesis 2:23-24 reads, *"Then the man said, 'This at last is bone of my bones and flesh of my flesh; she shall be called Woman, because she was taken out of Man.' Therefore a man shall leave his father and his mother and hold fast to his wife, and they shall become one flesh."*

Further, Ephesians 5:21-33 reads, *"Submitting to one another out of reverence for Christ. Wives, submit to your own husbands, as to the Lord. For the husband is the head of the wife even as Christ is the head of the church, his body, and is himself its Savior. Now as the church submits to Christ, so also wives should submit in everything to their husbands. Husbands, love your wives, as Christ loved the church and gave himself up for her, that he might sanctify her, having cleansed her by the washing of water with the word, so that he might present the church to himself in splendor, without spot or wrinkle or any such thing, that she might be holy and without blemish. In the same way husbands should love their wives as their own bodies. He who loves his wife loves himself. For no one ever hated his own flesh, but nourishes and cherishes it, just as Christ does the church, because we are members of his body. 'Therefore a man shall leave his father and mother and hold fast to his wife, and the two shall become one flesh.' This mystery is profound, and I am saying that it refers to Christ and the church. However, let each one of you love his wife as himself, and let the wife see that she respects her husband."*

3. Do you think these descriptions from Scripture can be lived out in a modern marriage?

_____

_____

_____

4. Have you ever listened to the wrong suggestion or advice in your marriage and suffered consequences for it?

_____

_____

_____

5. What should you have done to begin with?

_____

_____

_____

Kaiser states, "The Song of Songs is not a modern novel, nor is it a poem of love; instead, it is the Word of God proclaiming the beauty and purity of the marital experience in his master plan." However, how do we explain that King Solomon, as wise as he was, is the author who praises and teaches one man and one woman in an exclusive emotional and sexual relationship? We wonder about 1 Kings 11:2-3, ***"From the nations concerning which the Lord had said to the people of Israel, 'You shall not enter into marriage with them, neither shall they with you, for surely they will turn away your heart after their gods.' Solomon clung to these in love. He had 700 wives, who were princesses, and 300 concubines. And his wives turned away his heart."*** Because of this, we know that King Solomon mostly likely wrote the Song of Songs to be the ideal or correct example of what God intended for marriage. God's intent is for marriage to last in a close relationship like no other.

6. Is God's intention today for marriage to last a lifetime? Why?

_____

_____

_____

7. Do husbands and wives still feel like they belong to the other spouse?

_____

_____

_____

8. Why does this offend our current sensibilities as a culture?

_____

_____

_____

In Song of Songs 2:16, we read, *"My beloved is mine, and I am his; he grazes among the lilies."* This Scripture is the wife speaking about her husband. This level of surety in her position speaks loudly to the design being that marriages need to be centered on intimacy, commitment, and exclusivity. Further, in verse 4 it reads, *"He brought me to the banqueting house, and his banner over me was love."* This might seem like strange wording, but the wife's feeling of commitment, intimacy, and exclusivity is so strong that there is a flag carried around above her that says, "Love." He is mine! I am his!

In addition, Song of Songs presents marriage as a word picture or forecast of the marriage to come where the church will be married to Christ. Remember Ephesians 5:32, *"This mystery is profound, and I am saying that it refers to Christ and the church."* Akin writes, "The Song of Songs is to be read and preached in light of the entire biblical canon and through the lens of Ephesians 5:31-32, where we learn marriage is a mystery that 'refers to Christ and the Church.' It is through Christ that justified sinners find their home in a new Promised Land. The Song of Songs really does point forward to Christ." Just like the wife in the Song of Songs holds onto the love of a husband with such intimacy, commitment, and exclusivity so too, nothing can separate us from the love of Christ Jesus our Lord. In Romans 8:37-39 we read, *"No, in all these things we are more than conquerors through him who loved us. For I am sure that neither death nor life, nor angels nor rulers, nor things present nor things to come, nor powers, nor height nor depth, nor anything else in all creation, will be able to separate us from the love of God in Christ Jesus our Lord."*

9. For those of you who are married, do you agree that intimacy, commitment, and exclusivity should be a major focus of your earthly marriage? Why or why not?

_____

_____

_____

10. Are you comfortable accepting the intimacy, commitment, and exclusivity of our Lord and Savior Jesus Christ? Why or why not?

_____

_____

_____

GOD'S WAY

GOD'S DESIGN IN MARRIAGE, DEVOTION 1
Pastor Ryan and Cathy Story

Who would you go to for marriage advice? Some answers I am going to assume will pop to your mind will include parents, grandparents, pastor, author, or that sweet couple who has been married for 60 plus years who you see every Sunday at a Gathering. All of these would be amazing answers. Odd that no one said a polygamous, idolator who had God-given wisdom beyond any other person and chose a life serving the flesh rather than serving the Lord. Solomon is an odd choice for God to use to be the author of a specific poem about marriage, love, and sex. It would even be part of the inerrant Word of God that has been preserved since about the 10th century BC. For the next month, we have to ensure that when we look at this series we are less focused on our views of Solomon, marriage, intimacy, and sex, rather we are focused on what God's Word, the Bible, says about these things.

We live in a broken world. We live in a rebellious world. We live in a world where sin rules and self-glorification is more and more prominent. We live in a world that focuses more on self-worship, self-gratification, and self-exaltation. Many of us have fallen into these traps, and many of us know how damaging and broken the world can be, especially in the context of marriage. We should never use the brokenness shown in the Bible as a scapegoat for disobedience or use a person's sin as a reason to discredit their work for the Lord. Rather, the central character throughout the entire Bible is God. The truth about who God is, the truth about His power and love is saturated in every word of the Bible. Solomon fell victim to the exact same sin that destroys us today. Yet, in His mercy, God uses Solomon to pen one of the most pointed books in the Bible on the subject of marriage.

The subject of marriage is going to have a different heartstring tug for every reader of this book. Some who read this could be teenagers or young adults who are not at that point of being married. Some readers could be newlyweds who are forging into unknown waters. Some could be a married couple who are healthy and making their way through life. Some could be a married couple who are on the last lifeline and this book could be the "last hope" for their marriage that is bringing more hurt than joy. Some readers could be divorced or widowed. Too often when we look at the Bible through the lens of "what am I going to get out of this," we lose the beauty of the truth that is in front of us.

Solomon was given wisdom but could only scratch the surface of the beauty of what marriage actually is. Marriage is so much more than a man and a woman unifying their life together. Marriage is the ultimate show of Jesus. Paul writes in Ephesians 5:23-25, *"For the husband is the head of the wife even as Christ is the head of the church, his body, and is himself its Savior. Now as the church submits to Christ, so also wives should submit in everything to their husbands. Husbands, love your wives, as Christ loved the church and gave himself up for her."* While you may not be married, your marriage may not be where you feel God wants it to be, or you may feel the heartbreak of being without "the one that your soul loves," the truth about marriage is more about pointing to the Gospel of Jesus Christ. Song of Solomon ought not to point us to Solomon's failings or sexual past. The Song of Solomon is meant to point us to the truth that Jesus gave Himself up for our sins and as the church, we ought to love Him.

WORTH THE WAIT

GOD'S DESIGN IN MARRIAGE, DEVOTION 2
Pastor Ryan and Cathy Story

We live in a hurried society that wants things now. We live in a world where if we are going to order something online, we choose Prime so we can get it overnight. If we are in a grocery store, we will leave a lane to get into the lane that is seemingly moving faster. We get aggravated when our cell phones take longer than a second to load a website or an app. We lack the ability to delay any sense of gratification because, well, we are in a hurry and we want things now.

Song of Solomon chapter three is an amazing chapter to read for every single person regardless of age. The bride awakes in chapter three and realizes her beloved is nowhere to be found, so she searches for him. Song of Solomon 3:3-5 reads, *"The watchmen found me as they went about in the city. 'Have you seen him whom my soul loves?' Scarcely had I passed them when I found him whom my soul loves. I held him, and would not let him go until I had brought him into my mother's house, and into the chamber of her who conceived me. I adjure you, O daughters of Jerusalem, by the gazelles or the does of the field, that you not stir up or awaken love until it pleases."*

There is little question the bride desires to be with the bridegroom; yet, she is publicly searching for him. The bride has a deep sexual desire for the bridegroom. That desire is not sin, that desire does not make her a harlot, and that desire does not make her dirty. Sexual desire was given to us by God. (I will be writing more on this and the "Eden Hermeneutic" next week.) I love the last statement made in this section. Some believe this statement is Solomon entering the poem as a narrator, some believe it may be the bride groom, *"That you not stir up or awaken love unit it pleases."*

We live in such a hurried society and "we want it now," and because of that, we ruin what marriage is meant to be. Sex is meant to exist for God's glory and ought to be done God's way. We cheapen marriage because we have cheapened sex. We live in a world where "stirring up and awakening love" is viewed as self-discovery and healthy. God's Word, not some shame-filled purity sermon, tells us to not stir up passion until it is ready to bloom. This is not to avoid unwanted pregnancies or sexually transmitted diseases. The reason every person should wait for the right person is because of the negative effects that premarital sex can have on your spiritual life. Our bodies were given to us by God as a gift. That gift ought to be taken care of so one day, we can give that gift to the one who "our soul loved." You can argue all you want, but the inherent, error-free, preserved, powerful Bible shows us two young people who were absolutely in love with each other, who longed to be with each other physically. Yet, they did not stir up love until it was God's time.

THE STANDARD OF BEAUTY

GOD'S DESIGN IN MARRIAGE, DEVOTION 3

Pastor Ryan and Cathy Story

Truth be told, I am a bit of an awkward guy. I love to think of myself as a conversational artist, but that is hardly the case. When I was first pursuing my wife, I was put in the dreaded "friend zone" about three times. I think it has to do with, instead of just asking her out for coffee, I asked her if she would want to "meet at a local establishment for a preferable brewed Colombian bean." In retrospect, I see how that made me look like a crazy person. In my defense, I was attempting to be poetic.

Reading the poetry of any kind can be difficult. The Song of Solomon is no different. I love chapter 6. The bridegroom begins to dote on his bride. Being an awkward guy, I am weirdly drawn to each and every description he uses to describe his bride's beauty, *"Your hair is like a flock of goats leaping down the slopes of Gilead. Your teeth are like a flock of ewes that have come up from the washing; all of them bear twins; not one among them has lost its young"* (Song of Solomon 6:5-6).

Comparing a woman's hair to goats coming down from a hill is kind of awkward. Commenting on the fact that her teeth are all present and clean is kind of awkward. However, the sentiment behind both of those is amazing. Before the bridegroom comes off as weird, he tells his bride, *"Turn away your eyes from me, for they overwhelm me"* (Song of Solomon 6:5). Throughout these few verses in chapter 6, the bridegroom is madly in love with his bride and he is ensuring he vocalizes it. Even if it is awkward to our standards today, this man was overwhelmed by the beauty of the one who his soul loved.

From the moment a person weds, their spouse becomes the standard of beauty. This truth applies to both men and women. Song of Solomon chapter 6 is talking from the male perspective. Every husband reading this must take to heart that their wife is the standard of beauty until we see Christ face to face. Men, your wife is the most beautiful person in your life. She is the standard of attractiveness. This has to be true in our hearts as men. Unfortunately for men, we are mostly wired to seek beauty with our eyes. If it is not, that is when our hearts begin to wander, our eyes begin to look, and our marriages begin to crumble. If you are thinking, well I am no good with words, remember the bar for romance in the Bible is "you have nice hair" and " you have all your teeth and they are clean." Dollars to doughnuts you can speak some sort of encouragement to your spouse.

THE WAY THEY ARE

GOD'S DESIGN IN MARRIAGE, DEVOTION 4
Pastor Ryan and Cathy Story

Have you ever looked at your spouse and thought (or said), "Why are you the way that you are?" While typically a rhetorical statement, sometimes we really do wonder why someone is acting the way that they are. What causes someone else, especially our spouse, to make the choices that they make? You may question why your spouse loads the dishwasher in the wrong way, or why they fold the towels wrong. In these situations, there really may not be a wrong way of performing that chore, but we often look at situations or tasks and have a mental standard of how it should be done. We get caught in a trap of thinking we know the right way of doing something and it can frustrate us to no end when a task or interaction does not go the way we believe it should.

It can become easy to look at someone else, often our spouse, and to be bothered by the choices they make. With a spouse, we may look at those differences and allow the conversations in our minds to lead us down paths that we are really just too different from them. We allow how a dishwasher was (or was not) loaded, or selecting different settings on the washing machine or dryer, to drive us to negative thoughts. Those small mundane tasks can transform into continuing these negative thoughts, and at times, starting to wish that our spouse would change. We reason that if they were just a little bit different, if they made decisions more in line with our own, then our problems would be gone. We would no longer be as frustrated, and we would most certainly be happier. Except, the grass is not always greener on the other side, it is greener where you water it.

When we start having those thoughts of how we wish our spouse would make different choices or decisions, or if they could just change this one thing about themself, what we are actually doing is questioning the way God made our spouse. Isaiah 64:8 says, *"But no, O Lord, you are our Father; we are the clay, and you are our potter; we are all the work of your hand."* All of those little nuances that bother you about your spouse are a reflection of the way God made them. The way your spouse thinks is a sum of the life situations that God has walked them through. In Song of Solomon 5:10, the bride says, *"My beloved is radiant and ruddy, distinguished among ten thousand."* Her beloved is different! He is distinguished among ten thousand.

We have to remember to rejoice in the differences and rejoice that God made our spouses just the way they are. That ultimately, God had a plan when He brought you and your spouse together, differences and all! This does not mean there will not be situations that frustrate you, but at that moment try to thank God for the differences and the special way he made your spouse. Try to find an opportunity today to thank God for the unique way He made you and your spouse, and that in His sovereign plan you two are together.

LOST INTEREST

GOD'S DESIGN IN MARRIAGE, DEVOTION 5
Pastor Ryan and Cathy Story

Can you think of a time you lost interest in something you really wanted? As a child, maybe there was a toy or game you just had to have. How many days did it take for that interest to fade away after you got that item? Maybe you think about the job you were so certain was going to be so much better or just perfect, but a few months in you realize you do not like it as much as you thought you would. Just the other day, I was thinking about how in my late teens I decided to get into juicing. I read about the health benefits of juicing fruits and vegetables, I got books with recipes, and finally, I purchased a juicer. I brought it home and remember walking into the kitchen and telling my dad that I was going to start juicing things. His response to me was, "Is this a lifestyle change, or just something you are going to be into for a little bit." Well, more than twelve years later I can tell you that was just something I was into for a little bit. I could not tell you the last time I used that juicer, or honestly, if I still have it!

Paul David Tripp writes in his book, *"Marriage: 6 Gospel Commitments Every Couple Needs to Make,"* the idea that when we get married, the person who was once our greatest escape from reality becomes our greatest responsibility. That concept really struck me. When we first met we were so willing to go out of our way to spend time with, miss out on sleep, or spend money just to be with our significant other. However, then we get married, so often those same mentalities no longer seem to apply. The excitement of getting to see our spouse at the end of a long day just does not seem to be the same. The time and effort we were so willing to invest slowly seem to fade.

Song of Solomon portrays a couple whose passion and excitement for one another have certainly not been lost! Song of Solomon 2:16 says, *"My beloved is mine and I am his."* Their words throughout the book continue to express complete love and adoration for one another. There is no sense of lost interest between them! Song of Solomon 3:4 adds, *"Scarcely had I passed them when I found him whom my soul loves. I held him, and would not let him go."*

There may be many reasons we may start to feel as if the same love, interest, or spark is not in our marriages years after we have wed. The reality is that love grows, changes, and should deepen. Look for ways to show or tell your spouse that your interest is greater now than it was when you first met. If you are feeling like that same passion is not there, consider ways to reignite that spark. Try taking some time and writing out for your spouse (or telling them if writing is not your thing) how much they mean to you. Be descriptive, and have fun!

JUST YOU AND ME

GOD'S DESIGN IN MARRIAGE, DEVOTION 6

Pastor Ryan and Cathy Story

Have you noticed that in Song of Solomon there are very few people involved in the book? We see the bride, the bridegroom, and the "others." The focus of the book is on the bride and her beloved, which mirrors what should be important in a marriage.

One of the best pieces of marital advice, the advice I continue to share with others, was to not complain about my spouse to others. There are many times we will go and complain, but once a resolution has been made between one another, we do not always go back and tell the person we were complaining to how things improved. We move on, and while there is a resolution with my spouse, my friend would still maintain their negative viewpoint. This is not to say that we cannot seek godly wisdom or counsel, but if there is really an issue worth complaining or talking to someone about, it needs to be talked about with my spouse!

With God at the center, I can approach my spouse to have a conversation. That conversation needs to be just between the two of us. These conversations are meant to be constructive, helpful, beneficial, and honest. My spouse is someone I should and need to be able to clearly communicate with. Colossians 4:6 says, ***"Let your speech always be gracious, seasoned with salt, so that you may know how you ought to answer each person."*** In those conversations between us, we both have to think about our words. These are not meant to be times to cut each other down or tear each other apart, but the goal should be to better our relationship.

In Song of Solomon, we see the "others," their friends, bringing encouragement, but not weighing in their opinions. They are not questioning the bride about where her bridegroom is. They are not questioning the bridegroom why he would ever pick that woman. The friends are not used as emotional buffers until their loved ones return. The focus of the relationship is between the two involved in the relationship. Take some time today to think about your relationship. Are you running to others for problems or conversations that you should really be running to your spouse with? Are you being as open and bringing up topics, even the difficult ones, with your spouse? Remember to keep God at the center, and to let your words be seasoned with salt as you approach conversations you may have been avoiding.

SEX:
THE WORD
VS.
THE WORLD

DR. RANDY T. JOHNSON

"Awake, O north wind, and come, O south wind! Blow upon my garden, let its spices flow. Let my beloved come to his garden, and eat its choicest fruits. I came to my garden, my sister, my bride, I gathered my myrrh with my spice, I ate my honeycomb with my honey, I drank my wine with my milk." Song of Solomon 4:16-5:1

Douglas O'Donnell writes, "In the Song of Songs sex is at the center. I mean that literally. It's at the exact center of this Song. There are 111 lines from 1:2 to 4:15 and 111 lines from 5:2 to 8:14. So 4:16–5:1 is the centre of gravity, the heart of the Song … the central pivot around which the rest of the Song revolves, the centerpiece and crescendo. It's about sex!"

1. Did reading this passage make you blush? Why or why not?

_____

_____

_____

The Bible is very open about sex. God created sex to be beautiful, but mankind has tarnished it by worshiping the creation instead of the Creator. We need to understand that God promotes sex between one man and one woman within marriage.

2. Where are some areas where mankind has misused the gift of sex?

_____

_____

_____

The Song of Solomon is a most beautiful love poem. Its powerful language should not be so spiritualized that the physical passion it describes is stripped of its delight and candor. We need not be fearful of the topic. The world does not and should not set the rules.

Gods Allousvs. Condon.
Free Will

29

There are several areas where the world's view of sex is wrong.

- First, the world states that one should follow their heart.

I think we all have heard of people "following their heart." All too often people are in love with the concept of love. Jeremiah 17:9 says, **"The heart is deceitful above all things, and desperately sick; who can understand it?"** We need to trust the Lord and His Word, not our hearts and the world.

3. Where do you notice people follow their hearts without any logical consideration?

_____

_____

_____

- Second, the world states, "It is my body. I can do what I want with it."

As believers, we know this is false. In 1 Corinthians 6:18-20, we realize we are not our own, **"Flee from sexual immorality. Every other sin a person commits is outside the body, but the sexually immoral person sins against his own body. Or do you not know that your body is a temple of the Holy Spirit within you, whom you have from God? You are not your own, for you were bought with a price. So glorify God in your body."** When we accepted Christ as Savior, we made the decision to turn from serving ourselves to following the Lord.

4. How can we flee from sexual immorality?

_____

_____

_____

- Third, the world says, "It is okay to look at the menu as long as you do not place an order."

This is the concept that holds you can "check out" others as long as you do not take it any further. This worldly belief also likes to trick oneself into believing that pornography will not affect them. This is a slippery slope.

"I have made a covenant with my eyes; how then could I gaze at a virgin?" Job 31:1

"You have heard that it was said, 'You shall not commit adultery.' But I say to you that everyone who looks at a woman with lustful intent has already committed adultery with her in his heart." Matthew 5:27-28

"Finally, brothers, whatever is true, whatever is honorable, whatever is just, whatever is pure, whatever is lovely, whatever is commendable, if there is any excellence, if there is anything worthy of praise, think about these things." Philippians 4:8

5. How do these verses relate to the topic?

_____

_____

_____

Appreciate the beauty in the one God has given you. In the Song of Solomon, the man lovingly describes his bride's eyes, hair, teeth, lips, cheeks, and neck, and works his way down. He adores her. She completes him.

- Fourth, the world says, "You should check the teeth before buying a horse."

Keep eyes on Jesus -

how to be right   Lord Gives you way out.

I am not sure this is the most complimentary thing one can say, but this is one of the ideas behind premarital sex. Hebrews 13:4 summarizes it well, *"Let marriage be held in honor among all, and let the marriage bed be undefiled, for God will judge the sexually immoral and adulterous."* This rules out threesomes, the open relationship, someone on the side, friends with benefits, and unfortunately, the list could go on.

6. What other outlandish statements have you heard concerning reasons for having sex outside of marriage?

_____

_____

_____

- Fifth, the world says it is impossible to stay pure until marriage (or even in marriage).

In teaching this to teens, I would use a basketball analogy. I would tell them that the great coaches would encourage their players to miss all their free throws in practice so they would get all the misses out of their system. That way they would make them all in the game. Students would mock me (and rightly so). However, that is what the world teaches concerning sex. It is as if you can get all the sin out of your system. Instead, the Word supports the concept that discipline breeds discipline. If someone is undisciplined before marriage, why would one think that would change after marriage?

In 1 Corinthians 10:13, the Word says it is possible to stay pure, *"No temptation has overtaken you that is not common to man. God is faithful, and he will not let you be tempted beyond your ability, but with the temptation he will also provide the way of escape, that you may be able to endure it."*

7. What are some ways to avoid falling into temptation?

i We can Avoid

_____

_____

• Sixth, the world says, "God wants me to be happy."

The world wants to create God in its own image. There is this heresy that God wants us to be happy and we know how to get there. Actually, "happiness" (fulfillment, purpose, value, and meaning) come from pursuing righteousness. In 1 Thessalonians 4:3-8, we read, *"For this is the will of God, your sanctification: that you abstain from sexual immorality; that each one of you know how to control his own body in holiness and honor, not in the passion of lust like the Gentiles who do not know God; that no one transgress and wrong his brother in this matter, because the Lord is an avenger in all these things, as we told you beforehand and solemnly warned you. For God has not called us for impurity, but in holiness. Therefore whoever disregards this, disregards not man but God, who gives his Holy Spirit to you."*

8. In this passage, what is God's will for us?

_____

_____

_____

• Seventh, the world wants to hold one back by saying that if you have already sinned sexually, you should just do what you want.

God offers forgiveness. That is the message of the Bible. We sinned and broke our relationship with God. However, God sent His Son Who died for our sins (paid the price), rose again, and offers us forgiveness and life. In 1 John 1:9, we read, *"If we confess our sins, he is faithful and just to forgive us our sins and to cleanse us from all unrighteousness."*

9. What should one do who has fallen sexually?

_____

_____

_____

Scripture records from the earliest of times that a man and woman would leave the homes they were raised in and become one. There should be a ceremony with a celebration recognizing the unity. It is a bonding of soul mates that are coming together emotionally, mentally, spiritually, and physically. It is a very personal time. The Lord wants a couple to celebrate the unity.

In his commentary on the Song of Solomon, Douglas O'Donnell writes, "I want us to see that there is nothing so beautiful, continually fresh, and surprising, so full of sweet and perpetual ecstasy as love and lovemaking under the rules of our loving Maker. And I want us to see this in the light of the leprous nature of lust, the way the world so often thinks about sex today."

Finally, sex should not drive us from God (or become our god), it should point us to God. The world has us worship ourselves and we can never fulfill that void alone. The splendor of the marriage bed should help us realize that only God can bring a loving relationship. Douglas O'Donnell adds, "Christianity seeks to destroy in our hearts the idea of sex as a god and erects in its place the understanding that sex is a blessing from and a bridge to God." He later adds, "God gave us sex to arouse and satisfy a hunger for intimacy. Sexuality arouses a desire for union. Sexual consummation satisfies the desire, but it also mysteriously creates a hunger for more - not only for more sex, but also for a taste of ultimate union, the final reconciliation with God."

10. What areas in your life do you need to submit to the Lord? Have you given your life to the Lord?

_____

_____

_____

"So flee youthful passions and pursue righteousness, faith, love, and peace, along with those who call on the Lord from a pure heart." 2 Timothy 2:22

FOR MARRIAGE

SEX: THE WORD VS. THE WORLD, DEVOTION 1
Pastor Ryan and Cathy Story

God created marriage. That truth has to be known, understood, and lived out. Marriage is not an institution man came up with. Marriage was not created to put two people in a lifelong relationship of conflict, tension, and misunderstanding. Marriage is one of the most beautiful pictures we have to see God's mercy, grace, and love. Adam was alone, God saw that loneliness was not good. God put Adam to sleep and created Eve. Amazingly, God created women perfectly without Adam's input. When Adam awoke, Adam was taken back and glorified God by exhorting his bride. God conducted the first wedding ceremony. Then He commanded man and women ***"be fruitful and multiply"*** (Genesis 1:28).

God created marriage and within that marriage, God created sex for marriage. If we hold fast to the understanding of who God is, what God has created, and to live out God's will and plan for our lives we have to view sex as an activity that should only exist within marriage. When we view sex as our own personal outlet for pleasure, our means of finding worth, or our avenue of expressing our emotions, we are taking the gift that God has given us and turning it to worship ourselves rather than the Creator. Everything that is created was created for God's glory, that includes sex.

We live in a world that has lost its mind when it comes to sex. Advertisements, television, and social media are riddled with sexual imagery and innuendo and yet the church remains silent on this topic. Many people, inside the church and otherwise, have lost one of the most basic warnings we see about sex in the Bible. Song of Solomon 8:3-4 reads, ***"His left hand is under my head, and his right hand*** *embraces me! I adjure you, O daughters of Jerusalem, that you not stir up or awaken love until it pleases."*

Even in a moment of immense physical intimacy, the bride is being held by her love. There is a strong possibility both parties just had sex with one another, they are enjoying each other's company, and then as if out of nowhere, do *"not stir up or awaken love until it pleases."* It is as if Solomon while writing this realized his folly. His wisdom brought him to the truth that God created sex for His glory, not man's. Many of us view sex through a filter that is corrupted by sin. God has given us a gift, and it is up to every person to rely on the Holy Spirit to give us the self-control needed to ensure that we honor the gift of sex. Saving sex for marriage is old fashioned because it is how God made it in the beginning.

If you are reading this and thinking, "Welp, I missed." We serve a loving God that is capable of transforming our dead, sinful hearts into hearts that are full of life. Our lively hearts need to crave to be obedient to God and follow His Law (Ezekiel 36:26). We have a loving, forgiving, and merciful God.

If you have taken God's gift of sex and prematurely partook with a self-focused heart and if you feel shame, understand that it is not from God. I pray if you feel that, you would bring yourself humbly to the cross and ask for a new heart, and for a new desire to live a life that glorifies Him in all that you do.

"AND GOD SAW IT WAS GOOD"

SEX: THE WORD VS. THE WORLD, DEVOTION 2

Pastor Ryan and Cathy Story

I mentioned last week about the Eden Hermeneutic. Hermeneutics is the theory and methods of interpreting the Bible. Now, it is always important to understand that God's Word (the Bible) is infallible and without error, not man's interpretation. Hermeneutics is amazing to dive deep into if you are looking for more understanding, engagement, appreciation, and application of the Bible. Eden was paradise on Earth. Eden was the place where God placed man, beast, nature, and eventually woman. The Eden Hermeneutic takes the initial aspect of God's Creation and we hold to the truth that God made all things in this universe good, perfect, and holy. God perfectly designed the intricacies of everything we see around us, from flora and fauna to molecules and stars; God said it was *"good."* God perfectly sculpted man from dust (Genesis 2:7) and perfectly made women from man's rib cage (Genesis 2:22-23). On the sixth day of creation, God said it was *"very good."*

Genesis 1:28 reads, *"Be fruitful and multiply and fill the earth."* God created sex. God's first command to man and woman was *"multiply."* One of the first conversations to exist in our universe was between Adam, Eve, and God; they talked about sex. The Eden Hermeneutic teaches us that everything in this world that God created was made good. There will be much to say about the warnings behind sex, sexuality, and sexual desire, but the reason we have those warnings is that Genesis chapter 3 happened. Sex was originally designed to fit within the God-ordained *"good"* like everything else in creation.

In Song of Solomon chapter 7:12, when the bride says to her husband, *"Let us go out early to the vineyards…there I will give you my love,"* we have to look at the act of sex (within the confines of marriage, and with God-honoring desire to be other-centric focused) as good. It is good to have sex within marriage. It is not gross. It is not dirty. It is good.

Sadly, we live in a world that is hyper-focused on sex. The sin that rules all of our hearts has taken the amazing, good gift of sex, and turned sex into something that God never intended it to be. We all know the dangers that are behind the topic of sex, but we must never forget that God made sex good and acceptable to His will for the universe.

LET'S TALK ABOUT IT

SEX: THE WORD VS. THE WORLD, DEVOTION 3
Pastor Ryan and Cathy Story

Differences in our upbringings cause so many variations in thinking, conversing, and acting. Think for a second about the past few interactions you have had with people. Whether that person is a spouse, child, friend, co-worker, neighbor, or a random encounter in public, you can likely think of differences that you have compared to that other person. The beginning of a marriage is such an interesting time, as you realize just how many differences you have with this person you have now committed yourself to! As we think about it today, there are people who find the topic of sex normal and easy to talk about. Then there are people who view the topic as one to avoid at all costs. As with most things, there are times and places where sex should be discussed.

All of Song of Solomon presents a very open conversation about romance, love, and quite descriptive physical descriptions between the bride and bride groom. It was interesting to read in a commentary by David Guzik, that for many, if they came across the early writing of Song of Solomon outside of the biblical canon, they would likely view this book as secular! However, 2 Timothy 3:16-17 reminds us, *"All scripture is breathed out by God and profitable for teaching, for reproof, for correction, and for training in righteousness, that the man of God may be complete, equipped for every good work."*

From the Song of Solomon, we can see the importance of speaking openly with our spouse about our romantic life. Most of the book feels like we have walked in on a very private conversation. Too often we may want to skip over this portion of Scripture as we wonder what in the world there is for us to take away from here. It can be so much easier to jump to the New Testament and be reminded of the good works that Jesus did, or the relatable writings of Paul. The question then begs, do we approach the topic of sex this same way in our marriage? Do we want to jump over it, talk about the kids, finances, meal plans, vacations, or really anything but sex? Maybe it was something you discussed in premarital counseling, so now you are good, and have no need to discuss sex with your spouse because you have already discussed it.

Song of Solomon is such a great reminder that we still need to have these conversations with our spouse. Notice the conversation is not with the friends nearby. While the conversation is completely open between the two lovers, it does not need or involve anyone else. The conversation about sex is one the world is more than willing to have, but oftentimes within the church and in our marriages within the church, we do not want to talk about it. Taking into account any differences you and your spouse may have, consider taking time to discuss sex and intimacy with your spouse today. Maybe it is a conversation you need to start and come back to, or maybe today really is not a good day. I challenge you to make the time to talk with your spouse about your intimacy and appreciation for how God has made your spouse.

INTERCHANGEABLE

SEX: THE WORD VS. THE WORLD, DEVOTION 4
Pastor Ryan and Cathy Story

Have you ever thought about how interchangeably we use words? We can say, "This pizza is awesome!" the same way we will say, "God is awesome!" You may say, "I love this food!" the same way you might say, "I love my spouse!" A book can be good, but that does not even come close to the goodness of our God. Clearly, no one would go about believing that you love food or books in the same way you love your spouse, children, or friends. Our words and actions work together to demonstrate what we say we feel.

Unfortunately, the world often wants to interchange priorities and passions in our lives. The passion and desire we should have for our spouse can seem interchangeable with the love we have for our children, or the requirements we have for a job. We can make sex, something that should be regarded as special and an incredible bonus to marriage, almost like a checklist item just like we do with assignments at work. The world wants to tell us that there just is no time for intimacy because that time is interchangeable with something else.

When you have a passion and desire for something, you talk about it. You share about it. It is like a spring overflowing out of your mouth. Matthew 12:34 reminds us, ***"For out of the abundance of the heart the mouth speaks."*** The bride says in Song of Solomon 7:10, ***"I am my beloved's, and his desire is for me."*** Would your spouse be able to say that about you? Can you say that you feel that same way about your spouse? Is your desire for one another?

The world will tell you that time, energy, and even your spouse, are interchangeable, but that is not what God tells us. When we marry, we become one flesh. The Old Testament mentions several times how they would go into their tents and *"become one."* We have to stop the lie that everything in life is interchangeable because some things just are not. Pizza places are interchangeable, and cars are interchangeable, but taking the time to show my spouse how important they are is not interchangeable. What flows out of your heart and mouth when it comes to your spouse? Are you excited to get home to them at the end of the day? Would others believe that your desire is for your spouse? Or does your desire seem to be for something else? Take time to consider if your spouse would be able to say Song of Solomon 7:10 in regards to your relationship. If you are not sure that your spouse could say that, what could you change in your relationship so that they can?

BIBLE VERSE FOR THE BEDROOM

SEX: THE WORD VS. THE WORLD, DEVOTION 5

Pastor Ryan and Cathy Story

When talking about sex, there is a razor-thin line between crass and profitable. I pray throughout these devotions I have not landed on the crass and offended, but I also hope I have been able to speak the truth in the reality we live in. This is a disclaimer. My heart for this devotion is strictly profitable and meant for building up.

Hobby Lobby is an amazing place. One of my favorite items they have is the Scripture verse wall decor. I enjoy going to different people's houses and seeing different Scripture wall decals. Depending on the verse, it can tell you a lot about the family. I have seen Ecclesiastes 4:12, Jeremiah 29:11, John 3:16, and Joshua 1:9. It is a blessing to see families rally behind Scripture as a household focus and a truth to be lived out.

I have met many people who have a Bible verse for their work ethic, workout routine, creative activities, raising their children, and even cooking. Many may not have a Bible verse for the bedroom. So often we do not like to put sex into our conversations when it comes to faithfully living out the Gospel. When the Word of God is not an authority in all areas of our lives, we tend to drift away from living how God intended. This is especially true with sex.

It is tragic when sex becomes detached from God. We live in a world where sex has become an individual pursuit and a personal idol. Seldom do we apply God's Word to our sex life. The sin that rules every one of our hearts elevates our pursuits to be the center of the universe. For many married couples, sex has become more of a "me-focused" act rather than a means to display the service and other focused practices of Christ.

God designed sex to be a place where a husband and a wife can both humbly serve each other. Philippians 2:3-4 says, *"Do nothing from selfish ambition or conceit, but in humility count others more significant than yourselves. Let each of you look not only to his own interests, but also to the interests of others."* 2 Corinthians 5:14-15 adds, *"For the love of Christ controls us, because we have concluded this: that one has died for all, therefore all have died; and he died for all, that those who live might no longer live for themselves but for him who for their sake died and was raised."*

We cannot discontinue the Bible in our sex life. Sex was created for good, and yet sin has caused it to become a ruling and controlling aspect of our lives. When this happens, the sin in our hearts hurts people. If your sex life is more about you, your needs, and your satisfaction, you are not thinking about your mate, you very well are spiritually damaging them. Humble yourselves to the Word of God, look at your heart, and ask yourself, "Is the way that Jesus asks us to live being lived out on the marriage bed?"

GOD'S PLAN FOR YOU

SEX: THE WORD VS. THE WORLD, DEVOTION 6

Pastor Ryan and Cathy Story

Sex is a topic that is very intimate and personal. Our culture wants people to think participating in a lifestyle full of sex is not a big deal. It is normal and sometimes even encouraged to be intimate with multiple people before you can really find "the one." While we look at and talk about how God has designed sex to be for marriage, there are those who may feel conflicted if their past did not always align with how they now look at God's design.

No matter our past, we can rejoice in Psalm 103:12 which reminds us, **"As far as the east is from the west, so far does he remove our transgressions from us."** When we go to the Lord for forgiveness, and we have repented (or turned from our sin), we can rest in the knowledge that forgiveness is ours. We have a fresh start, a clean page, and we now get to decide how we are going to move forward. We cannot change the past, but starting today, we can change how we live the rest of our lives. Our view of the future should not only include us but include the next generation that is being brought up.

In Song of Solomon 2:3-5, we see, **"As an apple tree among the trees of the forest, so is my beloved among the young men. With great delight I sat in his shadow, and his fruit was sweet to my taste. He brought me to the banqueting house, and his banner over me was love. Sustain me with raisins; refresh me with apples, for I am sick with love."** The bride is satisfied with her bridegroom. Contrary to the encouragement of the world, we can be satisfied with the one God has given us. We do not need to search recklessly to find this person. We can trust that in God's infinite wisdom and power, He will bring that person into our lives when He deems the time is right. This is a truth we need to make sure the next generation knows and understands: trusting that the Lord has a perfect plan for our lives. It can be very difficult to trust God when we feel lonely, insecure, or that God has not forgiven us. That seems to be when we take God's plan into our own hands and create more frustrations in our lives. Sarai tried to take God's plan into her own hands and created friction with Hagar; that friction is still evident to this day. Rebekah tried to take God's plan into her hands and ended up causing her favorite son to have to flee, never to see him arrive where God had promised. Whenever we become impatient and try to take God's plan into our own hands, all it does is create a mess. Trust that God has a plan for you.

We are reminded in Romans 12:2, *"Do not be conformed to this world, but be transformed by the renewal of your mind."* No matter your past, are these the truths you are working to live by now? Are these the truths you are working to teach and instill in those around you? It is so much easier to look at another person and say, "Jesus can and will forgive you," or "Trust God has a plan." Sometimes we need to be able to instill these truths in our own life.

LESSON THREE

DANGERS:
LITTLE FOXES

PASTOR JAYSON COMBS

At the beginning of 2004, my wife, Laura, and I bought our first home. She was a substitute teacher and I was a middle school student director. We were looking for a house that had walls that were not leaning. We bought our first house and then took the next three months to make it livable. Everything needed to be redone. At the time, this work was an exhausting and sometimes frustrating process. Oddly enough, nowadays we look back on those memories and both Laura and I are quite fond of the memories we were able to make.

One day, Laura mentioned wanting to have a garden. We had a sizable backyard, so I did not think too much of it and I figured I could make that request happen. The back corner of our backyard was a perfect spot; all I would have needed to do was remove one plant that was growing there. In all my life I had never seen a plant like this before. It grew in what I can best describe as stalks. It looked a little like bamboo but was way more flimsy. As I started removing this plant I realized the root system was huge. It took me days to remove most of it. The scary and frustrating part of removing this plant were a few days after I removed a sizable amount of this plant and its roots. It all started to rapidly grow back. It grew even out of the stumps that I removed from the ground. At that moment, I did what all of us do when we are trying to figure something out about anything. I Googled it. The more I read about the plant, the scarier it became. I came to find out that the plant was a "Japanese Knotweed." One person said on an online forum, "My dad battled Japanese Knotweed for 25 years. He has passed away, but the knotweed lives on."

I have told this story many times over the years. Just recently I had someone in the church tell me that they found out that some banks will deny mortgages on a house if the knotweed was present near the foundation of the house. The root system of this plant can wreak havoc on foundations and drain systems. It is crazy to think of the power of this little plant and the destruction that it can bring.

1. What are some small frustrations that have wreaked havoc or damaged your house?

_____

_____

_____

In the Song of Solomon, we learn about something small that would cause great havoc. It is the analogy of a little fox. Song of Solomon 2:15 says, ***"Catch the foxes for us, the little foxes that spoil the vineyards, for our vineyards are in blossom."***

Daniel Akin likens these foxes to little villains that have the potential to wreak havoc and destruction. He goes on to say that foxes "were notorious in the ancient world for damaging vineyards." Many believe the author is relating the destruction caused by these little foxes in a vineyard to the little sins that can creep into our marriage. Again Akin says, "Solomon knows the beautiful vineyard of marriage is susceptible to destruction when littles foxes sneak in without our noticing them." Charles Spurgeon once said, "A great sin cannot destroy a Christian, but a little sin can make him miserable."

In this lesson, we will not come close to naming all the little foxes that can creep into marriage and destroy it, but we will take time to look at three foxes that have ruined many marriage's vineyards.

Fox 1: The Little White Tail Fox

This may be the sneakiest of all the foxes. This is the fox that justifies sexual sin. Daniel Akin says, "It is seductive and dangerous. It will destroy your life and you won't even see it coming. Sexual sin is appealing; it promises pleasure and happiness and can even deliver it for a little while but then it kills you. Sexual sin may cause you to walk away from God or at least redefine God as someone who is okay with your sin."

The seductive woman in Proverbs chapter 5 says, "We will not get caught." Yet the destruction is not only the sin of adultery, the destruction comes with a little lie. Proverbs 7:18-20 says, *"Come, let us take our fill of love till morning; let us delight ourselves with love. For my husband is not at home; he has gone on a long journey; he took a bag of money with him; at full moon he will come home."*

John MacArthur points out five ways to catch the fox before it ruins the garden:

- Avoid looks. Proverbs 6:25 says, *"Do not let her capture you with her eyelashes."*

2. What are ways we must protect our eyes? How can you help protect your spouse's eyes?

_____

_____

_____

- Avoid flattery. Proverbs 5:3 says, *"For the lips of forbidden women drip honey."*

3. What is flattery and why is flattery so dangerous when it comes from the wrong place?

_____

_____

_____

- Avoid thoughts. Proverbs 6:25 adds, *"Do not desire her beauty in your heart."*

4. What are common foxes of your thought life that in the end will destroy your marriage?

_____

_____

_____

- Avoid rendezvous. Proverbs 7:7-8 says, **_"A young man lacking sense, passing along the street near her corner."_**

5. What are some places you should avoid?

_____

_____

_____

- Avoid the house. Proverbs 7:25 says, **_"Let not your heart turn aside to her ways; do not stray into her paths."_**

6. What lies are you allowing to live inside your heart?

_____

_____

_____

If we do not deal with the Little White Fox and we let it hang around in the vineyard of our life it will eventually destroy the vineyard. Likewise, if we allow these lies into our marriage it is a matter of time before the vineyard of our marriage is in ruin.

Fox 2: The Red Fox

This Red Fox is an angry fox. This fox is small and quick but when you try to catch it, for some reason, this red fox does not just run away in fear, it becomes aggressive and attacks.

Ephesians 4:30-32 says, *"And do not grieve the Holy Spirit of God, by whom you were sealed for the day of redemption. Let all bitterness and wrath and anger and clamor and slander be put away from you, along with all malice. Be kind to one another, tenderhearted, forgiving one another, as God in Christ forgave you."*

7. How would you define bitterness, wrath, anger, clamor, and slander?

_____
_____
_____

8. How can this fox destroy the vineyard of your life?

_____
_____
_____

9. How can a married couple catch the Red Fox?

_____
_____
_____

Fox 3: The Quiet Fox

I cannot help but start this section by saying, "What does the fox say?" Wherever you are in life you can have fun with that nostalgia. The Quiet Fox is the one that is silent and does not communicate. If ever there was a destructive sin in a relationship, it is the sin of poor communication. We could spend months on communication but here are a few key thoughts that we must understand.

Ephesians 4:15 says, *"Rather, speaking the truth in love, we are to grow up in every way into him who is the head, into Christ."*

10. How are we told to speak? What does truth without love look like in a marriage? What does love without truth look like? Do you struggle with one more than the other? Why?

_____

_____

_____

James 1:19 says, *"Know this, my beloved brothers: let every person be quick to hear, slow to speak, slow to anger."*

11. What must we do with our ears? What is one thing your spouse would say hinders your ability to hear well?

_____

_____

_____

James 1:22 continues, *"But be doers of the word, and not hearers only, deceiving yourselves."*

12. What must we be doing with the Word of God?

_____

_____

_____

Ephesians 4:29 says, *"Let no corrupting talk come out of your mouths, but only such as is good for building up, as fits the occasion, that it may give grace to those who hear."*

13. What should our communication do? What corrupt talk do you allow to hurt your communication in your marriage?

_____

_____

_____

Proverbs 15:1-2 adds, *"A soft answer turns away wrath, but a harsh word stirs up anger. The tongue of the wise commends knowledge, but the mouths of fools pour out folly."*

There are only three little foxes, but we must learn to catch them. We must learn to protect the beautiful garden of our marriage.

DANGER OF
THE GRANDIOSE

DANGERS: LITTLE FOXES, DEVOTION 1
Pastor Ryan and Cathy Story

Romantic comedy movies have created an unrealistic expectation of the world. In most romantic comedies there is one sweeping grandiose gesture and everything is happily ever after. As I have watched most of these movies, I have laughed at the unrealistic expectation that is created for men. The "moral of the story" for most of these movies is that if you mess up enough, all that is needed to rectify the situation is to sing a song in front of crowds of people, run through an airport, stand outside a house with a boombox blaring a song of significance, or (my personal favorite) leaving an important business client to walk into a room saying the perfect words that rectify all the past pain that has happened. This unrealistic expectation has created in the minds of many that a healthy relationship is built on one moment, and that just is not true.

When the bride in Song of Solomon cries out, *"Catch the foxes for us, the little foxes that spoil the vineyards, for our vineyards are in blossom"* (Song of Solomon 2:15), the bride is crying out for the husband to catch the small little things that are destroying the vineyard's fruitfulness. At this moment, the bride is not crying out "save the vineyard," or "patch the hole in the fence that is allowing the foxes to get in." The bride is calling to start with the small problems in order to solve the bigger problem. It was not one sweeping gesture that was going to solve the bride and her beloved's problem; it was going to be solving multiple, small problems in order to bring a resolution to the main problem.

In marriage, too often we overlook the small. We fall for the romantic comedy trap and believe the lie that if we take the right vacation, plan the right date night, buy the correct gift, or do the correct amount of laundry all of our marital problems will be caught. The reality is marriage is built in the small everyday moments. Small moments of tenderness, small moments of encouragement, small moments of service, small moments of affection, and small moments of prayer make a huge impact. Big moments are great, but the sturdiest wall is built brick by brick. In the same way, what seem to be the biggest destroyers of marriages, intimacy, friendship, and joy inside a marriage? It is the small moments of tension, frustration, unforgiveness, bitterness, and harsh comments. In the same way that a strong marriage is not built by one grandiose action, more often than not, a marriage does not disintegrate with one action; it is several small actions that mount to destruction.

The bride's call to "catch the small foxes" is an amazing truth for every husband and wife to cling to. One of the biggest dangers that exist inside a marriage is the overlooking of the small moments that are hurting our marriages. On the optimistic side of things, this is also a means to begin seeing health return to a relationship. Make the most of small moments. Instead of putting all your energy, and bank account, into an amazing vacation, put time into the small moments.

DANGER OF SUCCESS

DANGERS: LITTLE FOXES, DEVOTION 2
Pastor Ryan and Cathy Story

The opening statement of Song of Solomon is, *"Let him kiss me with the kisses of his mouth"* (Song of Solomon 1:2). This sets the tempo for the entire book. The bride, bridegroom, and townspeople (which is a bit weird that they were so invested in this relationship, but I digress) proceed to dote on the love that is between these two. After sweet talking to each other with imagery of all of the flora and fauna they could think of, the bride turns her attention away from the bloom of the vineyard of their relationship and focuses on foxes. I feel for this man. Imagine sweet talking your wife, gazing into her eyes, complimenting her beauty, being stunned at the beauty of what God had created, and all the while she is responding in kind and she looks at you and says, "There is still laundry that needs to be done." That is a definite mood killer!

The transition from, "I see your face everywhere I look" (Song of Solomon 2:14) to *"Catch the foxes for us, the little foxes that spoil the vineyards, for our vineyards are in blossom"* (Song of Solomon 2:15), is like taking an interstate off-ramp at 70 miles per hour. However, the more you look into this moment, the more beautiful it becomes. The bride and bridegroom are lost in the bloom of the vineyard that is their relationship. There is romance, longing, intimacy, tenderness, encouragement, and vulnerability. All the things are going right. Yet, what does the bride focus on? It is the small foxes. These are the little foxes that snuck into their vineyard to spoil. Now we could conclude that the bride was only focused on the problems. I see it in another way. She is not looking for the negatives, she is ensuring that the vineyard of their love is always in bloom.

Ralph Mastron once said, "One of the biggest threats to success is success." When things are going great, we seldom put the effort into ensuring that things continue in that direction. When our marriages are healthy, it is easy to become lax on praying together, encouraging each other, and taking the time to be tender with one another. When things in the vineyard of our marriages are in bloom, it is easy to fall into the rut of thinking that blooming is how it will always be. Success can create a false sense of security that "the good times will always last." Paul David Tripp says, "Perhaps the greatest danger to a good marriage is a good marriage; because, when things are good, we are tempted to give way to feelings of arrival and forsake the attitudes and disciplines that have, by God's grace, made our marriage what it has become."

By no means am I wishing everyone to have a rocky marriage, but the willingness to work is the essential attitude to ensure that marriage remains strong and Christ-centered. Success can erode the awareness that there are foxes in every vineyard. Sin is constantly knocking at all of our doors. Our need for Christ is ever present. While it is possible to have a healthy marriage, the inability to see foxes sneaking under the fences can create havoc on the health of a marriage. When we are unhealthy, we know we need to go to a physician for care. Seldom do we go to the physician for a checkup when things are healthy.

DANGER
OF THOUGHTS

DANGERS: LITTLE FOXES, DEVOTION 3
Pastor Ryan and Cathy Story

Have you ever caught yourself in an out-of-control thought pattern? One word, one action, and one thought, can cause our thoughts to completely unwind. Sometimes all it takes is one statement from our spouse and we find ourselves pondering, analyzing, and fuming over that thought the rest of the day. In the same way, sometimes those statements are good, uplifting, and helpful. Then we spend all day thinking about those statements in a positive way. In the situations where the statements we stew over are not positive, edifying, or uplifting, we can allow our thoughts to begin tearing down ourselves again and again. Our minds have the ability to create situations that have never happened. Our minds have the ability to take something that has never been spoken and portrays that as the most absolute reality.

When the bride in Song of Solomon says, ***"Do not gaze at me because I am dark, because the sun has looked upon me"*** (Song of Solomon 1:6), she may have created a false narrative in her mind. Her darker skin may have been attributed to working out in the fields, which at the time would have indicated lower social standing. The bride may have questioned if she would be able to be loved in return, or questioned if she was worthy enough for the one she loved. She could have insecurely thought through scenarios of how he may respond to her if she tried to approach him. We get a brief glimpse of how her thoughts may have unwound and caused her to question herself in his eyes.

This glimpse into the mind of the bride is like a glimpse into our minds as well. We question ourselves, we end up doubting ourselves, and we wonder what others will think, or how they will respond to us. We follow the rabbit trails in our minds of what someone else is going to think, and how they are going to respond or react to us, and we then speak and live based on these assumptions. Just as the bride seemed to feel a need to preface her words to her beloved, we often feel the need to preface and explain our words and actions to others. We sit on others' responses to us and rerun those situations through our minds.

In marriage, parenting, and life in general, keeping control of our thoughts and minds is so important. We are reminded in Philippians 4:8, *"Finally brothers, whatever is true, whatever is honorable, whatever is just, whatever is pure, whatever is lovely, whatever is commendable, if there is any excellence, if there is anything worthy of praise, think about these things."* We keep control of our minds to help us live confidently in the way God has created us.

THE BEAUTY OF HARDSHIP

DANGERS: LITTLE FOXES, DEVOTION 4
Pastor Ryan and Cathy Story

I have never met a married couple who has not had their fair share of hardships. It can be hardships that are self-induced or a Job-like storm the couple goes through together. I know I was under a fierce sense of denial of that before I got married and thought that my marriage would always be healthy. If I worked hard enough and planned well enough, I could create a wall so amazing it would keep all the little foxes out. I made that wall. I kept my eye on influences that would be a detriment to the health of my marriage and I kept that portion of the wall high. When I first got married, I thought that all hardships to enter my marriage would be caused by external threats. The truth we all have to come to is the biggest threat that will bring hardship into your marriage is not from the external, it is from the internal.

So often in our relationship with Jesus, we view external influences as the biggest threat to that relationship. Now we have to know, that those external influences are dangerous! Sex, vulgarity, cynicism, fear, consumerism, envy, and pride run rampant within media. The world we live in views God's Word less as truth and more as a guideline that can be accepted or rejected. We live in a constant state of hurry that does not allow us time to spend the time to **"be still, and know that I am God"** (Psalms 46:10). As much as we can claim all of those influences are the biggest hardship we see in our walk with God, we have to come to the realization that those are not the biggest threat. The biggest threat to your walk with God, the number one influence that brings hardship into your life, is the sin that resides inside your heart. We cannot build a wall to protect our marriages from hardship, because most of the time we are the ones who create the hardship.

Hardship is inevitable in this life. We live in an amazing time. Jesus has come and died on a cross for our sins to restore humanity's relationship with our creator. It is such an amazing act of grace and restoration when we call upon the name of Jesus for the saving of our souls and renewal of our lives! However, Jesus has not returned for His bride, His church. We live in this "in-between" state where we are not with Jesus in Heaven, where there is no sin, but we are not bound by living in our sin. So while we all live in this "in-between" we will have hardships because the sin that dwells in us is constantly trying to pull us to the sin that is externally in the world. Why do we see hardships in marriage? It is because of sin. It is not external forces that are to blame. Hardship in life is because we are living in a way that is contrary to how God has called us to live.

Every marriage will go through hardship. However, the beauty of hardship comes when our struggle leads us back to God. In 1 John 1:9, we read, *"If we confess our sins, he is faithful and just to forgive us our sins and to cleanse us from all unrighteousness."*

DANGER
OF ASSUMING

DANGERS: LITTLE FOXES, DEVOTION 5

Pastor Ryan and Cathy Story

The whole book of Song of Solomon is so greatly expressive. Both the bride and the bridegroom, her beloved, go back and forth explicitly expressing their love and passion for one another. Their communication is clear to one another and nothing is left to assume. When we leave others to assume what we meant, or we assume that someone else understands, we leave a lot of room for error and confusion. Clear communication, saying what we are thinking and feeling, is so important to any relationships that we have.

Consider a few examples of how assuming can lead to problems. Maybe you had just finished cleaning, you turn around and a freshly dirtied cup is now left in the sink. You might assume that your spouse or child is being selfish, thinking only of themself, and not respecting that you just took the time to clean the kitchen! Your assumption now has you starting to feel upset with them. Think of another scenario, maybe you are at work and asked for someone to get back to you on something. After a day or two without hearing back from them, you might begin to assume that they have forgotten what you needed, or maybe you begin to assume that they are not trustworthy to follow through on what was needed of them. Now, imagine saying something unkind to someone you care about. In a moment of frustration, you said something that you know really was uncalled for. Instead of going back to apologize, you may start to assume that whoever you were speaking to knows you, so they clearly know you did not mean what you were saying. You will just move on from that situation assuming they will move on too and everything will be alright. Are you seeing the problem with making assumptions?

Proverbs 13:17 reminds us, *"A **wicked messenger falls into trouble, but a faithful envoy brings healing."** Ask yourself if your communication with others is clear. Is what you say bringing healing, removing assumptions, and expressing yourself in a respectable way? If you compare yourself to the way the bride and bridegroom communicate throughout the Song of Solomon, would your communication be that clear? Do you make sure you say, especially to those you love and are close to, what should be said to help build them up and encourage them? As you think about your communication, do you find that you leave others to assume what you mean, or do you find yourself assuming the intent of others?

Try to find a few people you can express your thankfulness, love, and gratefulness to this week. Be clear with them about why you are thankful or why you love them. Take the chance to apologize, or make sure a loved one is not having to assume your intent or meaning behind what you have said. Use the Song of Solomon as a guide for clear talk without assumptions.

DANGER OF PICKING YOUR CORNER

DANGERS: LITTLE FOXES, DEVOTION 6

Pastor Ryan and Cathy Story

The other day my son said to me, "Mom, I made a new friend! We have something in common, so I think that means we are friends now." In my mind I thought, exactly son, this is a true basic building block of having a friend. We find something we have in common with someone and we can build from there. While there are times we befriend others who may not share many, if any, similarities, sometimes that difference is exactly what draws people together. You are so opposite that their interests really intrigue you. You become drawn to doing something so out of the ordinary from your normal, it then becomes a common interest between you and this person!

In Song of Solomon, we see "others" responding throughout the book. These friends are encouraging, uplifting, and standing with their friends in love. The people they had picked to be in their corner were supportive of them and they could be found shouting encouragement! Who we pick to have in our corner supporting us matters! Proverbs 18:24 says, *"A man of many companions may come to ruin, but there is a friend who sticks closer than a brother."* As adults, many of us can talk about the importance of having that friend that sticks closer than a brother, or someone who you know is always there for you. Evaluating if our friendships are truly Christ-centered is still an important task.

If your corner is full of people, who are great friends, and love you immensely, but do not push you closer to Jesus, your corner may not be as great as you think. Proverbs 13:20 says, *"Whoever walks with the wise becomes wise, but the companion of fools will suffer harm."* Picking your corner is not just about filling your corner with people of common interest, while important, your relationship with God is much more important. A friend is one who can and will speak truth into your life. Sometimes truth is hard, and sometimes the truth is unpleasant. A true friend will not forsake speaking the truth in love.

In the Song of Solomon, the words of their friends spurred them on in their love for one another. Their friends did not bring them down or tell them to question their love. Their friends are a source of blessing and life, not a distraction. Consider who you have put in your corner. Are there people who are enjoyable people, but do not push you closer to Jesus? You do not have to unfriend them, but maybe they are not the strongest basis of friendship. Are your friends pushing you closer to Christ and offering biblical wisdom? If you cannot find these people in your corner, maybe it is time to make some adjustments to create a more God-centered life!

LESSON FOUR

DELIGHTS

PASTOR JOSH COMBS

Admittedly, the music on my iPhone is pretty eclectic. It is a weird combination of 90's Christian music, movie and Broadway soundtracks, Disneyworld music, rock music we have played in prisons, and songs I listen to when I exercise. Fun fact: Pastor Jayson (author of the previous study guide) and I both love cheesy 70's and 80's love songs. When we ride together to lunch, you might see us weirdly sitting at a stoplight jamming to some really corny music. I know, it is weird. On my phone, I also have *"Barry White's All-time Greatest Hits."* Honestly, I cannot remember why I downloaded the entire album, but I did. At times I will make my kids squirm by playing *"Can't Get Enough of Your Love, Babe"* or some other ridiculous song super loud in the kitchen. It never fails to embarrass them and I love every minute of it. This album from the late 1970s and the Song of Solomon both have themes of love, desire, romance, and sex. Frankly, both can, at times, make me blush.

As we approach the Song of Solomon or the Song of Songs, it is important to remember that what we are reading is a song. Solomon was a prolific writer. According to 1 Kings 4:32, **"He also spoke 3,000 proverbs, and his songs were 1,005."** Some commentators see the Song as the best of those songs written by King Solomon. We might make the mistake of reading the Song as just poetry on the page, but it was a song to be sung. Imagine printing the lyrics to your favorite song and just reading them, without any rhythm or melody. It would be flat and boring. It would be humorous if you knew the way the lyrics were structured to rhyme or flow, where rhythm changed, and the melody came through. Song of Solomon (or the Song) is a love song.

1. What is your favorite love song?

_____

_____

_____

Over the last 2000 years of Christian history, the Song of Songs has been the subject of countless commentaries, sermons, and interpretations. Early in Christian history, the church, sadly, was shaped by the dualism of Gnosticism and Plato's philosophy that anything earthly was evil and spiritual things were good. Basically, the body and spirit were divided, one being evil and the other good. This split caused the church to, in many different ways, demonize sex. By the early 300s, the church, according to commentator Douglas O'Donnell, viewed celibacy as the highest form of spirituality and even looked down on sex within marriage. On a side note, I wonder how those critics thought they got here. Anyway, this demonizing of sex caused the church to interpret the Song as allegorical (God and Israel or Christ and the Church), political, and in other bizarre ways. Essentially the Song was allowed to be interpreted anyway except sexual. A biblical dilemma arises if you remove the Song from the Bible or as Tremper Longman warns, "desex" the Song. We are left with very small amounts of verses in Scripture praising sex within marriage and massive amounts of verses warning against the dangers of sex (fornication, adultery, and homosexuality).

2. In your own experience with the church and Christians, have you seen sex demonized? If so, how?

_____

_____

_____

A key to combating a poor interpretive approach to the Song is a return to Genesis, specifically the Garden of Eden. Read Genesis 2:15-25. There we find Adam and Eve married, naked, and not ashamed (Genesis 2:25). What is even more foreign to our broken minds, is that God conducts the wedding with a naked bride and groom, and God is not embarrassed, ashamed, or blushing. God is the creator and designer of marital intimacy. God created sex and said it was good. As a matter of fact, **"God saw everything that he had made, and behold, it was very good"** (Genesis 1:31). I would wholeheartedly agree.

Within the Song of Solomon, we see many beautiful parallels with Genesis chapter 2 and the perfect world Adam and Eve lived in prior to the fall. In my opinion, the Song is the return to the Garden of Eden that a Christ-centered marriage delivers. As one of my friends put it one time, rather than being Hedonistic about sexual pleasure, this is an Edenistic view of pleasures that God has created. That is the unique purpose of the Song of Songs within the books of the Bible (the Canon). It is God's way of praising **"the way of a man with a virgin"** (Proverbs 30:19). It is a married couple returning to the true intimacy of Eden with God joyously present.

There are four important themes of delight in erotic poetry of the Song of Solomon.

Love

Some authors see in the poetry of the song a story, while others reject the narrative approach and see the book as a collection of ancient love songs. Regardless of where you land, love is a major theme in the book.

Okay, time for a quick contest. Take out a blank sheet of paper. Set a timer for three minutes and list a number of songs with the word "love" in them. After the time expires, read each of your lists out loud. The point should be really clear that there are lots and lots and lots of songs about love! However, "What is love?" (Also a song title.) Love, trust, friendship, and passion are all intertwined, not separate in this beautiful song.

3. Song of Solomon 8:5-7 attempts to describe love. List some of the descriptions.

_____

_____

_____

"To be loved, to be loved, what a feeling to be loved." It is not to be lusted after but loved. In the Song, this couple expresses their love in words, actions, names ("my love"), feelings, and longings.

4. How would you describe love?

_____

_____

_____

5. Read 1 Corinthians 13:4-8. How does the Apostle Paul describe love?

_____

_____

_____

Three times in the Song of Solomon, the writer warns against awakening love before it is time because it is a powerful force. (Cue Huey Lewis singing, *"The Power of Love."*) See Song of Solomon 2:7; 3:5; and 8:4. The point the author is making is to keep love locked down until the proper time because once it has been stirred up, there is really no putting it back away. Conversely, when it is time, stir up and awaken love all you want. It is wonderful and one of God's gifts to a married man and woman. O'Connell writes, "Patience now, passion later."

Desire

Most books of the Bible seem to have a target audience. It is not that the book is exclusive to that particular group, but it is important that somebody outside of the target audience recognize who the book is primarily written for. This helps avoid miscommunications that we call misinterpretations. Within Wisdom literature, Proverbs seems to be targeting boys with the repeated refrain, *"My Son,"* while the Song of Solomon seems written to girls of or near marrying age with the repeat, *"Daughters of Jerusalem."*

When we first meet the female character of the book, sometimes called Shulamite (6:13), she seems insecure and uncertain of her beauty. As the book progresses from one sexual encounter to another with her husband, her confidence grows. Her desire for him grows congruent with his expressed desire for her. She feels safe and confident.

Read her description of herself. (Song of Solomon 1:5-6)
Read his description of her. (Song of Solomon 4:1-5; 7:1-9)
Read her description of him. (Song of Solomon 5:10-16)

6. Why are words of praise and desire to your spouse important?

_____
_____
_____

7. What often happens when words of praise and desire are absent?

_____
_____
_____

Availability

I asked my wife to look over this lesson as I was writing it. I had only completed the introduction and had my four points typed out. She scrolled down and came to this section. She said, "This is the do it when you want to and when you don't want to" part of the lesson. She is not very wordy, but she knows how to make a clear point. Like desire, availability comes from stability and reliability. Faithfulness and being truly present lead to greater sexual availability of your spouse. In chapter 5, the couple at the center of this incredibly romantic song seems to have a miscommunication which leads to some unmet expectations. There is some debate whether 5:2-7 is a true narrative or a nightmare. I do not really feel the need to make an interpretive decision either way, because the book is a song or a poem. Either way, dream or "reality," there was trouble in paradise. Read Song of Solomon 5:2-7. It seems that the man expected intimacy, while the woman was annoyed he came home so late. She warms up, but by that point, he has given up.

8. In your marriage, have you had sexual miscommunications?

_____

_____

_____

9. In your marriage, have you had sexual unmet expectations?

_____

_____

_____

10. Have you or how did you address these miscommunications and unmet expectations?

_____

_____

_____

Sexual availability is also about ownership. That may seem like a heavy term and even out of place, but read on, I will try to clarify.

She says…

"My beloved is mine, and I am his." (Song of Solomon 2:16)

"I am my beloved's and my beloved is mine." (Song of Solomon 6:3)

"I am my beloved's and his desire is for me." (Song of Solomon 7:10)

She is clearly saying, "He belongs to me and I belong to him." These passages are a precursor to 1 Corinthians 7:4-5 where Paul writes, *"For the wife does not have authority over her own body, but the husband does. Likewise, the husband does not have authority over his own body, but the wife does. Do not deprive one another."* Earlier Paul wrote, *"You are not your own, for you were bought with a price. So glorify God in your body"* (1 Corinthians 6:19-20). If you know Christ, the Lord has purchased you through His work on the cross. Then if you are married, He, in essence, gives the ownership of your body to your spouse.

11. How can you more sacrificially make yourself sexually available and more generally available to fulfill your spouse's needs?

_____

_____

_____

Satisfaction

The stunning, erotic poetry of the Song respectfully reveals this couple's most intimate moments. It is not graphic for the sake of shocking its readers, but it is naked and not ashamed. The echoes of Eden are evident in the theme of a luscious garden, vineyards, and orchards woven through the song. The symbols of creation are liberally used. Horses, flocks, gazelles, and mountains (that cannot be found on maps) are all used to illustrate this couple's passion and satisfaction with each other. The most erotic and Edenistic, in my mind, is the garden metaphor.

He says, *"A garden locked is my sister, my bride, a spring locked, a fountain sealed."* (Song of Solomon 4:12)

He says, *"Awake, O north wind, and come, O south wind! Blow upon my garden, let its spices flow."* (Song of Solomon 4:16)

She responds, *"Let my beloved come to his garden, and eat its choicest fruits."* (Song of Solomon 4:16)

He responds to her, *"I came to my garden, my sister, my bride."* (Song of Solomon 5:1)

(This sequence reminds me of an incredible duet. Think of Marvin Gaye and Tammy Terrell, *"Ain't no Mountain High Enough."*)

"My beloved has gone down to his garden to the beds of spices, to graze in the gardens." (Song of Solomon 6:2)

He likens her to a garden and not just any garden, but *"my garden"* and she refers to herself and her body as *"his garden."* Gardens take a lot of dedication and work. The lovers of the Song lavish on each other acts of love that are exclusive! This exclusivity has led to immense pleasure and satisfaction. It is what Daniel Akin calls a "sexual symphony." What we mean by exclusivity is the now old fashion idea of monogamy. We are talking about fidelity, commitment, and marriage.

God's plan of *"they shall become one flesh"* (Genesis 2:24) is meant for greater pleasure, not less.

12. How does exclusivity lead to greater satisfaction?

_____

_____

_____

Longing

Without any hesitation, the Song of Songs is a celebration of human love, wonderfully expressed within the context of biblical marriage. As we saw in lesson 1, marriage has a deeper meaning. The love of a man and woman and vis versa is a preview pointing us to the main attraction. This does not empty marriage of meaning, rather it gives it its full expression. Paul writes in Ephesians chapter 5, that the mystery of a man and woman becoming one *"is profound, and I am saying that it refers to Christ and the church"* (Ephesians 5:32). Do not abandon the foundational fact that the Song of Solomon celebrates God's good creation of sex, but take some of the themes and see their full expression in Christ.

13. Read John 15:13. How did Jesus describe love?

_____

_____

_____

14. How did He show love?

_____

_____

_____

Sex is a God-given preview of the ultimate satisfaction we will have when we see the Lord face to face. John Piper said, "God is most glorified when you are most satisfied in Him." Read Psalm 16:11.

15. Are you satisfied with Christ?

_____

_____

_____

Eugene Peterson in the Message, paraphrases Song of Solomon 3:1, writing, **_"Restless in bed and sleepless through the night, I longed for my lover, I wanted him desperately. His absence was painful."_** On the surface, the woman of Solomon's greatest Song was lonely and longing for her love. If we see this portion of the Song illustrating longing (which there are lots of love songs that are really longing songs), we recognize that as humans we have deep longings in our souls. We long for meaning, purpose, fulfillment, truth, friendship, love, and satisfaction. That emotion of longing is God-given. It is built into the fabric of who we are. God hardwired us to long for Him, because He and He alone ultimately satisfies. Saint Augustine wrote, "You have made us for yourself, O Lord, and our hearts are restless until they rest in You."

One day, our "wedding" day will come. The groom, Christ, will return to take His bride to the home that He has been preparing (John 14) and we will be forever with the Lord. Revelation talks about the great Marriage supper of the Lamb, a grand and eternal wedding reception. If you have been to some of the receptions I have been to that might sound like the opposite of Heaven, but this will not be endless waiting, bad food, or awkward conversation. This will be the culmination of all we have been longing for. It will be *"pleasures forevermore"* (Psalm 16:11).

Sources
"The Song of Solomon: An Invitation to Intimacy" by Douglas Sean O'Donnell from the "Preaching the Word Series."
"NICOT," *"Song of Songs"* by Tremper Longman III.
"Christ Centered Exposition Exalting Jesus" in *Song of Songs*, by Daniel Akin.

REMIND THEM

Pastor Ryan and Cathy Story

People love to be told how well they are doing. You may like hearing how beautiful and clean your home is, how nice your outfit looks, how much great work you put into that task, or how amazing your children are turning out! We all love compliments! I have this habit of when I cook, I like to ask my family just how much they enjoyed the meal. I can ask multiple times in one sitting if they liked the new recipe, if would they change anything, or if I should make it again. Chances are I will still leave the table feeling as if I would be alright if I was told again how good the meal was. We all love positive feedback. We live in a society where we can post pictures online where our friends and family can share their adoration, likes, and love of whatever is happening in our lives. As people, we love to hear that others are pleased and delighted with us.

Consider for a moment just how often in the Song of Solomon we read the bride and bridegroom reminding one another of their love. He reminds her in Song of Solomon 1:8, ***"O most beautiful among women,"*** and she reminds him in 5:10, ***"My beloved is radiant and ruddy."*** These are two of many examples of times they expressed adoration for their loved ones. These two lovers leave no room for doubt about how they feel.

Think about how long it takes for you to start doubting something. If I think about my cooking with my family, if I have not heard someone say within the first few bites that the meal tastes good, I am probably already starting to doubt if it turned out very well. Have you ever posted a picture on social media and then contemplated taking it down because no one had said anything about it within a few minutes? Doubts can creep in so fast! Ephesians 4:27 reminds us, *"And give no opportunity to the devil."*

Do not hesitate to remind your spouse, or any loved ones, just how much you love and delight in them. Challenge yourself to go beyond just liking the shirt they are wearing today. Remind them. Tell them. Tell them again, and then again. I would guess that Song of Solomon really could have kept going, that there would be more they could have, and probably did say, to one another. Live your marriage like a sequel to Song of Solomon, but it is you and your spouse. Remind them how and why you love them and after you have done that, remind them again.

WHO YOU ARE

DELIGHTS, DEVOTION 2
Pastor Ryan and Cathy Story

Song of Solomon leaves its readers with many questions. While there are thoughts and ideas about this book in Scripture, many answers just are not known. One aspect that is abundantly clear would be that the bride and bridegroom genuinely delight in the one they love. It seems pretty safe to say, you cannot read through these eight chapters and deny that fact! The bride looks at her bridegroom and delights in everything about him. She is broken-hearted when he is not there with her. In Song of Solomon 5:8, she says, *"I adjure you, O daughters of Jerusalem, if you find my beloved, that you tell him I am sick with love."* Among the bridegroom's many responses to his love, Song of Solomon 7:6 writes, *"How beautiful and pleasant you are, O loved one, with all your delights!"* Their adoration for one another is something they express time and time again.

With so many unknowns from this book, we might picture different scenarios. One scenario could be that clearly this is a young married couple, they still hold all of that whimsy and wonder that is so common early in marriage. Can we imagine this couple still being this delighted with one another years into a marriage? While love certainly should deepen and grow as the marriage progresses, there tends to be less of the whimsy, wonder, and constant flattery that often exists in the early stages of being with a loved one.

Daily routines, monotony, and annoying habits can seem to erode away at some of the initial delights we may have first felt as a couple. That does not mean that appreciation is lacking, but it seems so common that married couples lose some of the wonder they once held with their spouse. Consider when was the last time you genuinely thought and prayed through delighting in your spouse. We can quickly get caught up in focusing on the negative and frustrating aspects of our relationship (and they are there!), but that is one thing we do not see ever happening in Song of Solomon. The bride is never expressing frustration that her bridegroom is gone, but rather a sadness at the fact that he is not there. The bridegroom is not just satisfied with coming home, greeting his bride, and telling her she looks nice today; rather upon seeing her, he showers her with words of adoration. If you find your mind wanting to drift to negative thoughts regarding your spouse, work to pull your mind back to the things you delight in about your spouse. When you are able to mentally find what you delight in, then work on taking opportunities to text, call, and say those things to your spouse at every chance you get.

DELIGHT IN PROTECTION

DELIGHTS, DEVOTION 3
Pastor Ryan and Cathy Story

Song of Solomon chapter 3 is about the time many believe that the wedding between the bride and the bride groom is about to take place. In an amazing show of pomp the bridegroom, Solomon, sends a carriage and his personal guard to pick up his bride. Song of Solomon 3:7-8 reads, *"Behold, it is the litter of Solomon! Around it are sixty mighty men, some of the mighty men of Israel, all of them wearing swords and expert in war, each with his sword at his thigh, against terror by night."* This could be looked at as an extreme act of possessive ownership and toxic masculinity that Solomon is isolating his bride from the world. Nowhere in Song of Solomon is that the case. The truth is that Solomon knew that his bride was worth protecting and put his best foot forward to ensure she was protected.

In marriage, both husband and wife need to protect the delight they have for one another. We talked extensively about foxes last week. This week as we talk about our delight in our spouse, we have to ensure we are sending *"sixty mighty men"* (metaphorically speaking) to ensure that delight in our marriage is protected. At times we may need to protect our spouses from themselves and the blind spot they may have. At times we may need to protect your marriage from the "tyranny of the urgent" and the "relentlessness of hurry" and we may have to have the "quality time" conversation. At times we may need to discuss what we say "yes" to because we are spending more time with in-laws or friends than our own families. If there is a delight in your marriage, then take a page out of Solomon's book and send protection to ensure that delight is preserved and safe.

You might be reading this and thinking, "I have no or little delight in my marriage." Sadly, at some point, the *"sixty mighty men"* were not sent out. There is always hope when there is Jesus. We are not defined by our past mistakes and have the opportunity to "fix" (with the leading of the Holy Spirit) the areas in our marriage that we have lost our delight in. The best way to begin to protect the delights of your marriage is to start sending out the troops. Start small. Discuss with your spouse and figure out the delight that is most missed. Begin to pray about how you can begin to enjoy that delight again. Protect your spouse from shame, protect your spouse from time, protect your spouse from themselves, and protect them from whatever forces may be bringing them down.

VERTICAL DELIGHT

DELIGHTS, DEVOTION 4
Pastor Ryan and Cathy Story

It would be hard to imagine when two people choose to get married their desire is to have a marriage that is full of tension and strife. Sadly, almost every couple goes through a moment or a season where their marriage is not how God intended it to be. Gentle answers are replaced with snips and quips. Moments of admiring the beauty and uniqueness of our spouse are replaced with criticalness. Communication is replaced with silence. A once warm communion is replaced with a cold cohabitation. No one while walking down the aisle says to themselves, "I think in less than two years, I want to constantly be at odds with the person I am committing to love and to hold."

There are problems inside every relationship because every person in the world has a problem. Every person, outside of Jesus, was or will be born with a sinful heart. Sin causes us to focus solely on ourselves. The primary lie that Satan used on Eve in the Garden was that by eating from the Tree of Knowledge of Good and Evil, she would *"be like God"* (Genesis 3:5). The sinful desire of our hearts distorts every relationship we have, including the one with our Lord, by drawing us to a place where self rules. Any time there is tension in any relationship, if you search deep enough, the sin of pride is there.

When pride is ruling a person's heart, it destroys the relationships we have with people, and it destroys the relationships with God. Any tension we may encounter in our marriage with the other person can only first be solved by ensuring the vertical relationship with God is healthy. If there are tensions in your marriage, the only way to solve them is to first ensure there are no tensions in your walk with Jesus.

Also, we cannot properly delight in our spouse if we are not delighting in the Lord. It is impossible to delight in the uniqueness of your spouse if you do not see them as a perfectly created being. You cannot delight in your spouse in times of second-guessing, if you do not believe that God, in His infinite wisdom and His perfect plan, joined you and your spouse together. In order to properly delight in your spouse, you have to delight in the Lord.

Psalm 37:3-5 says, *"Trust in the Lord, and do good; dwell in the land and befriend faithfulness. Delight yourself in the Lord, and he will give you the desires of your heart. Commit your way to the Lord; trust in him, and he will act."*

PUBLIC AND PRIVATE

DELIGHTS, DEVOTION 5
Pastor Ryan and Cathy Story

Can people tell you delight in your spouse? Can your spouse tell you delight in them? The beauty of the covenantal relationship of marriage is that it is more than lovemaking. Inside the marriage, there is service, sacrifice, commitment, loyalty, and friendship. A husband must understand that while privately he shows his wife tenderness, devotion, and friendship, he also must do this publicly as well. This goes for wives as well.

Song of Solomon 8:1 says, *"Oh that you were like a brother to me who nursed at my mother's breasts! If I found you outside, I would kiss you, and none would despise me."* We read the closeness of this relationship between husband and wife. *"If I found you outside, I would kiss you"* is full of public displays of affection, and yet that is what a married couple should be. We have to focus on the *"I would."* She is not saying she is kissing him, but she wants to. PDA is frowned upon in public, and that was also the case in Solomon's time. All through Song of Songs, we read the *"others"* speaking of how much the bride and the bridegroom loved each other. Their love was publicly known, but they were not offensive with their love. Despite the fact that the couple was not physically intimate, the *"others"* could still tell that they were in love. Can people tell you delight in your spouse? Can they tell that your spouse is *"the one that your soul loves?"* (Song of Solomon 3:4) Can people see the warmth, tenderness, service, sacrifice, loyalty, and friendship that ought to exist inside of marriage? A great measuring stick to tell if you are delighting in your spouse is how would people say you delight in your spouse? Do they hear affirmation or complaining? Do people hear friendship or tension? Do they hear warmth, coldness, or even worse silence?

On the other side of this coin, does your spouse know you delight in them? Song of Solomon 8:2 adds, *"I would lead you and bring you into the house of my mother - she who used to teach me. I would give you spiced wine to drink, the juice of my pomegranate."* Note the phrase, *"bring you into the house."* Inside the marriage, intimacy, service, sacrifice, commitment, loyalty, and friendship all must be seen inside the house, in a spot of privacy. The amazing aspect of this verse though has to do with the notion of the *"house of my mother - she who used to teach me."* Inside of the home is an amazing place to teach children what intimacy, service, sacrifice, commitment, loyalty, and friendship look like. To rephrase that question, do your children know you delight in your spouse? While there are aspects within the marriage that are "behind closed doors," an overflow of that delight ought to be seen by others, especially our children.

DELIGHT

DELIGHTS, DEVOTION 6
Pastor Ryan and Cathy Story

If you were to pull out (or pull up if it is on your phone) your weekly or monthly schedule, how often is time specifically set aside to spend with your spouse? So often our days and schedules get filled quickly with work, sports, exercise, driving, and a whole list of additional tasks, but one area that often gets neglected is our marriages. While we may delight in our spouse, it may feel challenging to actually set aside time to show that. Time with our spouse often becomes the leftover portions of our week or those few minutes between when the last kid finally goes to sleep and you have not quite closed your eyes to sleep yet. While it is important to express and say our delight, it is just as important to show that we delight in our spouse as well, and one of the greatest ways to do this is with time!

With any relationship, we know that putting in quality time is key. It is hard to imagine any friendship, relationship, or marriage that is able to grow, let alone thrive, without the effort of putting time in. The word effort is used purposefully there, we have to make an actual effort to set time aside to spend with those we care about. Throughout the Song of Solomon, as we read their expressions of love for one another, we can see the importance of the time they are actually together. In Song of Solomon 5:4-6, *"My beloved put his hand to the latch; and my heart was thrilled within me. I arose to open to my beloved; and my hands dripped with myrrh, my fingers with liquid myrrh, on the handles of the bold. I opened to my beloved, but my beloved had turned and gone. My soul failed me when he spoke."* We can hear in the bride's words how thrilled she was at her beloved returning home, and upon not finding him at the door any longer her soul fails within her. The strength of the words thrilled and failed is so noteworthy. Not only is she happy, glad, or relieved that he is home, she is thrilled. I view that word as one with excitement and joy, something you have waited for and are so glad to receive. Then the opposite of this, when he is gone, her soul fails within her. She is not just disappointed or sad, but she is deeply saddened at the fact that he is no longer there. Would you consider similar emotions at the prospect of your spouse coming and going?

While his words certainly stuck with her, and while I would guess she knows how much she is loved by her beloved, it was the prospect of him physically being there with her that brought her heart so much gladness. There are many things in life that want to get in the way of us being able to spend time with our spouse, in the same way, these things want to get in the way of us spending time with God. Making and proposing that time to be alone and be together is pivotal for any relationship.

Look for days and ways to make time to spend together. Put a day on the schedule. Maybe finances make it difficult to afford a sitter, consider looking for other families you could swap watching kids with. Maybe you are not comfortable leaving your kids and need to plan a late evening date at home by doing something to make the evening special. You and your spouse may consider going for a walk through your neighborhood or the local park if you are not wanting to spend a lot. Get creative with a way to purpose time with just your spouse doing something out of the ordinary! Make that time a priority to remind your spouse just how much you delight in their company, the same way the bride and bridegroom delighted in being with one another.

OUR MISSION

Matthew 28:19-20: *"Go therefore and make disciples of all nations, baptizing them in the name of the Father and of the Son and of the Holy Spirit, teaching them to observe all that I have commanded you. And behold, I am with you always, to the end of the age."*

REACH

At The River Church, you will often hear the phrase, "we don't go to church, we are the Church." We believe that as God's people, our primary purpose and goal is to go out and make disciples of Jesus Christ. We encourage you to reach the world in your local communities.

GATHER

Weekend Gatherings at The River Church are all about Jesus, through singing, giving, serving, baptizing, taking the Lord's Supper, and participating in messages that are all about Jesus and bringing glory to Him. We know that when followers of Christ gather together in unity, it's not only a refresher it's bringing life-change.

GROW

Our Growth Communities are designed to mirror the early church in Acts as having *"all things in common."* They are smaller collections of believers who spend time together studying the Word, knowing and caring for one another relationally, and learning to increase their commitment to Christ by holding one another accountable.

The River Church
8393 E. Holly Rd. Holly, MI 48442
theriverchurch.cc • info@theriverchurch.cc